GINA CORRIGAN

miao textiles from
china

University of Washington Press
Seattle

First published in 2001 by The British Museum Press
A division of The British Museum Company Ltd
46 Bloomsbury Street, London WC1B 3QQ

Published in the United States of America
by the University of Washington Press,
PO Box 50096, Seattle, WA 98145-5096

ISBN 0-295-98137-7

Commissioning Editor: Suzannah Gough
Designer: Paul Welti
Cartographer: Olive Pearson
Origination in Singapore by Imago
Printing and binding in Singapore by Imago

COVER: Detail from a woman's festive jacket from Leishan and Laijiang county. (See pages 78-9)
INSIDE COVER: Detail from bead embroidery from Taijiang county.
PREVIOUS PAGES: Detail from the central panel on a baby-carrier from near Guiding county.
THESE PAGES: Detail from bead embroidery from Taijiang county.

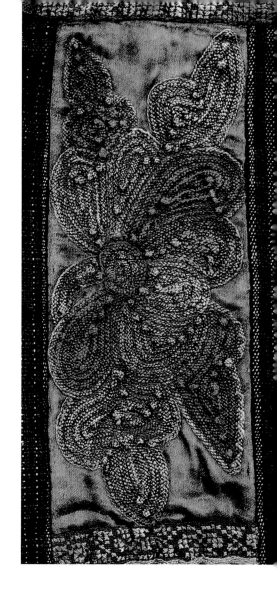

contents

introduction

ORIGINS OF THE MIAO

The textiles in this book are those of the
Miao people of Guizhou province, which lies
in the subtropical zone of south-west China.
Migrants into this area, the Miao are thought
to have lived originally in the Huang He
(Yellow River) basin, some 5,000 years ago.
According to legend, they were beaten in battle
by the Yellow Emperor and had to migrate
south to the middle reaches of the Chang
Jiang (Yangtze River), possibly 4,000 years
ago. By the Qin–Han period (221 BC – AD 220)
they had migrated to what is today western

Hunan and south-east Guizhou, and later to
south Sichuan. But pressures such as the
presence of rival Han settlers and established
indigenous groups, and imperial troops
pushing from the north, meant that the Miao
had constantly to seek new regions in which
to live. The problem was exacerbated by the
fact that the Yunnan–Guizhou plateau, an
extensive area of karst limestone with
rounded bare mountains, was largely
unsuitable for cultivation.

When Guizhou became an administrative
province under the Ming dynasty in 1413,
consolidation of imperial rule was ensured by
military invasion of the tribal areas, as well as
subjugation of the Miao and other minorities
and encroachment on to their land. The Miao,
who by then were in central and southern
Guizhou and eastern Yunnan, were thus
forced to continue migrating — into Thailand,
Laos and Vietnam.

In south-west China, according to the
1992 census, there were seven million Miao,
approximately four million of them living in
Guizhou province. Today they live peaceably
alongside the Han and other minorities, but
in the nineteenth century there were many
bloody Miao uprisings against the Han. The
Miao and other tribal peoples resented the
influx of Han settlers, and objected to high
rents and taxes. During this period of unrest
it is suspected that nearly five million people

A timber-framed Miao village beside paddy fields in Taijiang county.

died out of a total population of seven million. Abject poverty persisted, especially among the Miao, and observers in the first half of the twentieth century have told of the Miao being dressed in rags and of their children having to share clothes. Even today, many Miao live below the poverty line.

The Miao can be divided into four main dialect groups and many subgroups. The only language in which they can all communicate is Putonghua (standard Mandarin). There is no written Miao language, but a strong oral tradition. At the end of the nineteenth century the missionary Samuel Pollard devised a writing system for the Miao of western Guizhou, but the search for a common written language continues among Miao scholars.

Within the official Miao minority is a subgroup with its own distinctive culture and dialect, known as the Gejia ('Ge family'), who live in and around Kaili. Not wishing to be classified as Miao, the Gejia have been seeking their own minority status for many years, but as yet without success.

CLOTHING AND TEXTILES

Because the Miao were one of the later groups to arrive in Guizhou, they settled mainly in the mountains and rarely in the river valleys, which were already occupied by other minorities. Living as swidden cultivators with virtually no chattels, their most valued possession was their richly woven and embroidered festival costume. This not only identified them as belonging to a specific

Miao girls from Jianhe county wearing festive costumes and elaborate silver jewellery.

group but was also an indicator of family wealth, as was the wearing of several skirts or layers of jackets. Such traditions continue today — at festivals even the poorest families wear elaborate costumes, which can be considered the major living visual art form of the Miao culture.

Crafts such as decorative wood carving and pottery are not practised by the Miao, although specialized craftsmen, especially in the south-east, make superb silver crowns, necklaces, bracelets and plaques, which are stitched on to the girls' jackets. There is also a musical tradition of songs and lusheng bamboo pipe-playing by the men at funerals, festivals and weddings.

Miao people at a Lusheng festival near Liuzhi.

Since traditional costume is one of the most striking features of the Miao culture, it is hardly surprising that the Han, and foreign anthropologists, have come to identify the various groups within it by their mode of dress. There are probably eighty different Miao costumes in Guizhou (depending on how you categorize them) and local people have given nicknames to Miao groups according to particular aspects of their dress, such as Long and Short-Skirted Miao, White and Blue Miao,

and Flowery Miao. However, the Miao dislike these nicknames intensely and identify themselves according to their own dialect names.

The women's costumes are inventive variations on a basic theme. A long-sleeved jacket is worn over a full, pleated skirt that can vary in length from 27 cm (10½ in) to ankle length. Many groups have aprons, often worn front and back, and traditionally puttees or gaiters cover the lower legs. Garment construction depends on the use of narrow- weave, hand-loom cloth, which is rarely shaped by cutting, and there are normally no seams on the shoulders. Jackets and skirts are decorated with woven strips and with wax-resist and embroidery pieces. Each group has its own distinctive hairstyle. The baby-carrier, a prestigious accoutrement and part of the dowry, is elaborately decorated using the finest techniques. Men's costumes used to have design and decorative features similar to those of the women of their group, but much of this has now been lost.

FESTIVALS AND COURTSHIP

Young girls are taught by their grandmother and mother to spin, weave, dye and embroider, as every Miao girl needs a full traditional costume in which to attend festivals and to wear for her marriage. If a girl has not acquired these skills, her mother will make her costume, or, if she is too busy or her sight is poor, buy the various parts of it at the market, from Miao women who increasingly make an income from selling fabrics, woven ribbons and embroideries.

The major Miao festivals take place in the low agricultural season, between harvesting and planting the rice, or in the summer after the crops have been planted. Several villages, usually of the same costume type, get together to organize them. Families flock to these events, often carrying bundles of costumes on shoulder poles. Young unmarried girls try to have a new costume for each festival. Once at the site, they dress up in their finery, aided by their mothers. Some festivals go on for several days, and in remote areas, if it is too far to go home, families camp out on the hillside, where they heat pre-cooked rice and pork on small fires. There is always plenty of local alcohol to drink and related families and their friends will talk long into the night. Mothers often see their married daughters for the first time since their marriage on such occasions.

During the festival itself, the unmarried girls perform simple, slow-moving circle dances to the music of lusheng pipes, showing off themselves, their costumes and their jewellery to the unmarried boys. There are various distinctive courting rituals within groups. In some, liaisons can be made over the festival period, more formal arrangements being entered into later. Others involve complex rituals such as antiphonal singing, whereby the girls gather in someone's house after the festival and the boys court them from outside by singing through holes in the wall. The girls reply if they wish to make a liaison, and the boys are then invited inside.

It is said that unmarried Miao girls are judged by their future husbands on their ability to spin, weave, embroider and make an elaborate costume, the beauty and workmanship of which indicates their tenacity and industriousness. The number of skirts and jackets and the quality of the materials also show the wealth of the family. Poorer families, unable to allow their daughter much time off from agricultural pursuits, would have less ornate costumes.

BASIC FIBRES AND EMBROIDERY SILK

The base fibres used in Miao textiles vary from region to region within Guizhou. In the past, the main fibres for clothes were hemp or ramie, both of which come from the stalks of plants. Hemp (*Cannabis sativa*) is an annual, sown in March and harvested in August when approximately 2 metres (6 ft 6 in) high. The stalks are cut down, the leaves removed and the fibres teased out of the stems. After short lengths have been joined by splicing, the thread is wound into balls by the women. Some groups then twist it on a treadle-operated multiple-spindle wheel, presumably to give it extra strength. The yarn is boiled with ash and pounded until creamy white. It is then unravelled and balled, ready for weaving. Ramie (*Boehmeria nivea*) is a perennial, of which the stem is cut several times a year. The fibres are lifted and separated out from the stem with a metal tool. The process of making the yarn is similar to that of hemp, and from it a fine silk-like cloth is woven. Today ramie and hemp are increasingly woven with cotton or synthetics, although, for reasons of cost, pure hemp and ramie continue to be used in the poorer west and drier central areas.

Cotton crops will grow in the south of Guizhou, and here the Miao prepare their own cotton textiles by ginning, spinning and weaving. Increasingly, because of pressure to get the most out of the land, food crops are replacing cotton and therefore spun cotton from other provinces is being brought into the weekly markets. In the wealthier south-east, which is too damp for cotton-growing, both cotton yarn and manufactured woven cloth is sold at the markets.

In the north-west, which is more than 2,500 metres (8,200 ft) above sea level, women wear woollen felt capes and gaiters made by itinerant felters. Wool is also woven into the shoulders of the local hemp or ramie jackets for extra warmth.

Silk has traditionally been used as a base fibre by a few richer families in the south-east, especially in the Kaili and Huangping areas where it is possible to raise silkworms. One can still find Miao women selling the eggs and worms at the markets, and small amounts of silk continue to be produced for weaving. In 1996 a Miao woman told me that in the 1950s the local people used to make and dye their own embroidery silks, but now only the poor do this – others can afford to buy quality threads made in Shanghai.

LOOMS AND WEAVES

There is a rich weaving tradition in Guizhou, especially in the south-east. Two main types of loom are used. The more ancient is the body-tensioned loom, with the shafts usually operated by a rope around the foot. The other is the treadle-operated frame looms with up to four shafts. Most base cloth for skirts, jackets and trousers is woven in tabby (plain) weave. Lozenge twill weaves are common in the south-east, where an alternating float weave is also found, which is very highly regarded. The

A Miao woman with an embroidered baby-carrier watches another woman weaving ribbons on a frame loom, near Huangping.

hand-woven cloth varies in width from 32 to 38 cm (12½–15 in) and is normally dyed after weaving, although a few groups use dyed yarn to produce stripes and checks.

Supplementary weft techniques are common, in fabrics woven in wool, silk and cotton. Patterns for the decorative areas of garments and for baby-carriers are sometimes extremely complex, featuring birds, butterflies and geometric designs put in by hand. Weft-faced strips are also used on the back panels and decorative sleeve pieces of jackets. These are made on the large frame looms used for cloth production, as a piece of fabric 36 cm (14 in) wide, into which a spacer straw is

woven every 2–3 cm (¾–1¼ in) to create a sequence of strips. These are then cut out and sewn on to the costume, with the raw edges turned in. If a longer 'ribbon' is required — for example, for the front edges of a jacket — the selvedges are joined.

Some groups weave warp-striped coloured silk ribbons as decorative bands to be sewn on to skirts. Again several are woven at once, by leaving gaps in the warp. Also common are narrow (2.5–6 cm; 1–2⅓ in) warp-faced cotton and silk bands for tying gaiters, puttees and aprons, which are usually woven on smaller frame looms than those used for making cloth. Similar but wider bands are used as ties on baby-carriers. In Shidong an especially fine multicoloured ribbon is woven out of silk, with a warp float pattern on the front only. The Gejia use a body-tensioned loom to make waist and puttee ties, weaving with the warp tensioned on their big toes as they sit on the ground. Some Miao groups tie the warp on a post and tension the cloth beam around their body as they work sitting on a chair.

A particularly sophisticated weave has recently been identified on baby-carriers from the Geyi area (near Taijiang) in the south-east, although the details of this weaving technique are still speculative (Boudot 1994). Further interesting techniques will undoubtedly be revealed in other remote areas.

DYES AND CALENDERING
The most common dye in Guizhou is vegetable indigo, usually made by women, which is used

on all the base fabrics. It is made from the leaves of either *Strobilanthes cusia* or *Polygonum tinctorium*. *Strobilanthes cusia*, the most common plant used to make indigo paste, is grown every year from cuttings. In September the leaves are collected and soaked in barrels of water for anything from four days to two weeks, depending on the ambient temperature. Once fermented, the leaves are taken out and lime is beaten in to introduce oxygen. After several days the indigo pigment precipitates to the bottom. The water is then drained off and the dark blue indigo paste scooped out into baskets lined with leaves. If sealed, this can be kept all winter, and some families make indigo paste to sell at market.

Domestic dyeing is also usually done by the women, who reconstitute the indigo paste with ash and water in a wooden dye vat, found in most Miao households. Rice wine is added to encourage fermentation, which gradually reduces the oxygen in the vat. The dyer tastes the vat every morning to see if it is right for dyeing. Both hand-woven and bought fabrics are dyed, normally in the warmer months of September and October. They are dipped and aired many times to build up the dark blue colour, sometimes for as long as twenty-four days. A Shidong woman told me that between dye baths she immersed the cloth in soya-bean soup. She also boiled buffalo hide in water until soft and then used the liquid to dip the partially dyed cloth in between some of the indigo dye baths, which helped to stiffen the material. Cloth is also sometimes steamed and

beaten with a wooden mallet, according to information from Rongjiang.

There are many dyeing taboos. For example, if a pregnant woman goes near the vat, fermentation stops and the vat has to be started again. Sometimes lucky paper cutout figures are stuck on to the vat.

Shiny indigo-dyed cloth is prized by the Miao. Calendering is done by folding the material and beating it with a wooden mallet on a flat stone. Male professional dyers, and

Miao girls wearing festive dress and silver jewellery in Rongjiang county.

some families, use a huge 'rocking stone' in a technique also used by the Han Chinese. The cloth is put on a roller, which is placed under the stone. The man then stands on the stone, rocking from side to side while supporting himself on the rafters. Others rock the stone with their arms. In the south an even greater shine is achieved by dipping the indigo-dyed cloth in a liquid made from forest tubers and roots. After the cloth has been dried in the sun, egg white is applied and it is spread out and again left to dry, to a highly glazed finish.

Chemical dyes have been available in China since 1870, and today the dye vat is often spiced with a chemical to add depth to the blue colour and shorten the dyeing process. Home dyeing is common in Guizhou, but increasingly women take their cloth or yarn to be chemically dyed by the professional male dyers who come to the markets.

A particularly unusual effect is achieved by the Miao of Huangping, who colour their cotton and silk cloth green, using an aniline dye (which normally dyes purple) bought at the market in the form of green crystals. These are crushed, mixed with a little water to make a paste and painted on to the cloth. The material is then smoked over cypress branches and the process repeated several times. Next, it is folded and beaten with a wooden mallet. A shiny green colour is achieved, which eventually turns bronze in the open air. Other villagers dislike sitting next to these Miao on a bus, as the dye — not being fast — can rub a purple colour on to their clothes.

SKIRTS AND SKIRT PLEATING

One of the most important items of the Miao costume is the skirt, which is usually very full and pleated. There are three main methods of skirt construction. In one of these, anything from eight to around fifty vertical lengths of loom-width cloth are joined at the selvedges and pleated on to a waistband. Another method consists of joining several lengths of loom-width cloth horizontally to form a tiered pleated skirt that is attached to the waistband. Lastly, a single horizontal length of cloth is sometimes pleated to make a short skirt. The main pleating techniques are as follows:

▪ In hemp and ramie skirts, pleats are formed by gathering the first 10−20 cm (4−8 in) with 4−10 rows of stitching. The stitching is pulled in to the required waist size, producing a gathered effect, similar to smocking.

▪ Cotton skirt lengths are wrapped loosely around a cylindrical tube of wood or straw held in place by cords. The cloth is dampened with a starch solution, finely pleated with a small wooden stick or metal tool, and then dried in the sun. At this stage, some groups are said to steam the skirt in a large wok. Several lines of fine running stitch may also be added to secure the tops of the pleats. When the skirt is complete, the stitches in the back are often left in place, while the front is freed so that the wearer can walk comfortably.

▪ Tubular skirts of cotton, hemp or ramie that reach from waist to ankle, like a sari, are often pleated daily by the wearer and are held in place by a strong tie, as there is no waistband.

In the south, skirts are particularly finely pleated. Parallel lines are scored into the cloth with the fingernail and it is 'massaged' with the tips of the fingers until the pleats are sharp and concertinaed. Finally, the skirt piece is dampened, wrapped around a bamboo cylinder and tied on with cord, and allowed to dry.

Other women in the south fold the first pleat sharply to form a guideline. The material is then turned over and, with the thumb and forefinger of both hands, a second pleat is folded up to the first. This is repeated until there are ten pleats, which are rolled with the fingers to push them together. The skirt piece is then wrapped around a piece of bamboo and a starchy liquid is applied, which may include a solution made by boiling water-buffalo hide in water. It has been stated that the skirt is then steamed, although this process has not been witnessed. The finer the pleating, the more the skirt is prized, and women who pleat finely are greatly admired.

In another method, as much as 14 metres (46 ft) of single-width hand-loom cloth is placed on a trestle (the width of the cloth being the length of the skirt). Using a wooden spatula to pull in each pleat, the woman starts the pleating from one end, dampening the material she is working on with a red solution made from an unidentified root boiled in water. The day's work is allowed to dry in the heat of the house, and the next day the dried pleating is so firm that the woman is able to put it under a small wooden board and sit on it as she works on the next section.

WAX RESIST

Resist dyeing is a technique whereby designs are applied to a fabric using a non-absorbent substance (a 'resist') such as wax or rice paste, so that they remain the original colour after the dye solution has been applied. Widely used to decorate jackets, skirts and turbans, wax-resist dyeing with indigo is practised on hemp and cotton by many of the Miao groups. Unlike the Han Chinese, they do not use paste resist or stencils. Beeswax is the traditional resist, but increasingly paraffin wax is used, and in Huishui resin from the tree *Liquidambar formosana* is preferred. The wax is applied with a special tool made from two or three triangular pieces of metal bound to a bamboo stick. The width at the widest part of the metal varies from 5 to 40 mm ($\frac{3}{16}$–1$\frac{1}{2}$ in) and one waxer may have as many as twenty tools of different sizes. The heated wax, caught in a well between the metal pieces, is applied by slightly slanting the tool.

The group most expert at wax-resist dyeing are the Gejia, who produce complicated fine geometric patterns and bold floral motifs. Before waxing, they place the cloth on a board, smooth it with a stone and roughly outline the design using their fingernail. The liquid wax — kept in a pottery shard or bowl placed in a container of rice husks or ashes — is applied very hot so that the design penetrates the back of the cloth. After the cloth has been dyed in the indigo vat, the wax is washed off in hot water and is often re-used. The waxed design appears white on a blue ground.

The Miao women of the Zhijin area produce some of the technically finest work, while in central Guizhou several groups paint yellow, green and red natural or chemical dyes on their finished designs using hemp sticks or brushes. Waxing tools vary — a Miao group in the south use a chicken quill adapted to make a very fine painting brush, as well as pieces of bamboo. In the 1930s a missionary, Reverend Parsons, noted that porcupine quills were used in the north-west. The Miao in the north-west occasionally use a stitch-resist technique as well as wax resist on their hemp skirts. A stitch-resist butterfly design and a few bold floral designs have also been found in central Guizhou, but wax resist remains the most common method. However, it is thought that in the central south some Miao groups may be using stencils to make repeat designs for their skirts, as stencils were found in one village.

DECORATIVE TECHNIQUES AND STITCHES

Both jackets and skirts may be embroidered. This is usually done when the women are working outside, so it is more convenient for them to work on small pieces — for example, for the jacket, sleeve, line of the shoulder, back or neck edges — rather than the whole made-up garment. Many embroidery stitches are worked from the back, and the colours tend to be bright and vibrant, although in the south-east older women often overdye their clothes in indigo. Examples of the many different techniques used are given in the following list.

▨ Paper patterns are used extensively. Older, skilled women with knowledge of the designs draw them out on the top of ten to twelve sheets of paper, held together by twisted paper pushed through pinholes. The patterns are then marked or cut out with an awl, sharp knife or scissors and sold at the market. To use a pattern, it is tacked on to the cloth and the embroidery applied over the paper template, which remains on the finished jacket. The highly pictorial designs in Shidong are sewn in satin stitch. The work is embroidered in floss silk, finely stranded. To strengthen the silk and make it shiny, the embroiderer makes a paste of chewed locust bean and pulls the thread through it before use.

▨ The Miao living near Kaili are particularly good at working fish and bird designs in a folded silk technique. Starched silk ribbons are cut into small rectangles of 15 × 10 mm (⅝ × ⅜ in), two corners of which are folded down to form a triangle. These are then stitched on to the paper pattern through the points in overlapping layers. Two rectangles of a different colour may be folded together so that the triangle has a second colour inside. The same group also embroider floral designs in a knot stitch or modified chain stitch, using two needles. The design is outlined in white whipped cotton or in horsehair whipped with fine cotton thread, which is couched on.

▨ In Zhouxi, near Kaili, an unusual material referred to as 'silk felt' is applied to cloth to make tiny geometric motifs. Small pieces of silk felt are obtained by cutting the outside of a silkworm cocoon into small shapes, while larger pieces are said to be made as follows. Silkworms that are just starting to spin their cocoon are put on to a board in the dark. Unable to find anything to attach themselves to, they exude their silk threads over the flat surface. Later, the resultant mesh of threads is lifted from the board, washed, and patted into shape. This 'secret' process was recently verified by a foreign visitor who saw it being done, and this account is supported by Cheng Weiji, who writes: 'It was also the customary practice in ancient China to make silkworms spin silk on a smooth-faced wooden board instead of allowing them to make cocoons on a bundle of straw.' Dyed silk felt — which is very expensive — is cut into small shapes that are then further divided into thin layers. It is applied to the base cloth by fine oversewing. Coloured ribbons edge the various designs, and there is also an intricate metal edging, consisting of metal foil cut into minute dog's-tooth designs and stitched down.

■ A special technique in the south-east is the application of handmade fine silk braid in one or two colours. Measuring 5 mm (³⁄₁₆ in) across, it is made on a special braiding stool. Weighted silk threads are attached to a bar and the braid-maker crosses the threads over each other to form a braid, in a technique similar to lace-making. The number of threads used seems to vary between 8, 10 and 12, although odd numbers of 9 and 13 have also been seen. The braid is applied to sleeve pieces on to which paper patterns, usually with zoomorphic designs, have been stitched. It is either couched on flat, or pleated to produce a three-dimensional effect that is highly prized.

■ The papercut method of producing a geometric design involves drawing it on paper, cutting the pattern out and then placing this on top of the fabric. Pieces of material of various colours are cut into shapes and tacked under some of the design motifs, then stitched into place by sewing through the papercut.

■ It is said that a group of Miao in a remote valley near Jianhe stitch thin strips of a metal alloy on to their aprons and the back of their jackets, predominantly in a hooked geometric pattern. On the fringes and at the bottom of the apron, they wrap the alloy around a line of warp threads in which several wefts have been left out. The back apron is decorated with a subtle two-tone embroidery stitch between the metal patterns. This group's method is considered secret and I have not myself seen it being done, but their work has been collected.

■ Cross stitch is used extensively in a variety of geometric patterns.

SYMBOLISM

Rich symbolism is found in most Miao embroidery — telling the story of the Miao migration, representing their creation myths and their heroes, and echoing their animistic beliefs. In the south-east the motifs are dominantly zoomorphic, anthropomorphic and phyllomorphic, while in other areas they tend to be geometric. The symbolism itself will not be discussed here, as each group has its own legends, and, more importantly, one can only elucidate the true meaning of the motifs by speaking directly to the Miao in their own language.

TRADITION AND CHANGE

Most Miao women wear traditional costume on market day and on special occasions such as weddings, funerals and festivals, but those in poorer areas wear it every day, as they cannot afford to buy additional clothes from the market. Some women wear a mix of traditional dress and clothes bought at the market, and trousers and jackets are particularly popular for daily work.

Miao men sometimes have specific costumes for festivals, but mostly they wear 'Mao' suits, or Western-style clothes with perhaps a turban. This is probably because their experience is wider than that of the women — they are more likely to have attended school, and many will have served in the military or spent periods working in other provinces to earn extra money to support the family.

Miao girls are influenced by the clothes they see on television, now that electricity is available and even the poorest villages have at least one or two satellite TV sets. Only grudgingly do they wear traditional clothes to the market, as they much prefer to be 'modern', and some of the Miao costumes are impractical and uncomfortable. Most girls also prefer to wear their hair in a ponytail, as

many of the women have become partially bald as a result of traditional hairstyles. One group, for example, wear their hair scraped backwards and wrapped round a wooden horn tied into the back of their hair.

Some Miao girls are now beginning to attend school. Once educated, they either find jobs in nearby small towns or go to the Special Economic Zones on the coast to work. There they are exposed to the 'jeans and T-shirt' culture, and when they come home they no longer want to wear traditional costume.

Married Miao women with elaborate baby-carriers at a Lusheng festival, near Shuicheng.

Since the establishment of the People's Republic of China in 1949, local song and dance teams have been formed to promote socialist values and mores, as well as to emphasize cultural identity. These teams often perform in traditional dress before important guests at local government meetings, and the best are chosen to provide entertainment at sporting and cultural events, at both national and provincial level. In addition, a series of annual competitions are held to find the most talented teams. The winning troupes are invited to perform on provincial and national television, and they also promote China abroad. Although traditional dress was initially worn for such performances, it has gradually been adapted into a stage costume. Long skirts have been shortened and indigo-dyed costumes are embroidered with sequins and pearls. Local girls have emulated these alterations, as the song and dance teams are greatly admired and the performers envied.

Westerners have been visiting Guizhou since the end of the 1980s, when certain villages began to be chosen by the Government to be opened up to foreign visitors. These villages' song and dance teams entertain the tourists in costumes to which further subtle changes have been made, and even greater adaptation will come about as the domestic tourism market explodes and more villages perform before Chinese tourists with a taste for more exotic entertainment. Most tourists also want souvenirs, the Chinese often buying small good-luck trinkets to take home as gifts,

while the Westerners tend to choose pieces of traditional embroidery and items of costume. The 'open' villages provide an outlet through which women from other villages can sell their work, but the supply is not endless. Sadly, many Miao groups are beginning to make costumes of poorer quality, not only to sell at the market but to wear themselves.

Kaili is the major marketplace for the sale of traditional costumes. Here, over the past ten years, a network of Miao dealers has built up, who scour Guizhou for items to sell. One remote poor village is said to have given away at least ten festival costumes to a Miao dealer in exchange for a pig to feast on. The growing culture of private enterprise is epitomized by a Shidong woman who saved enough money to marry her daughter to a Miao man employed by the Transport Department in Kaili. After the marriage she went to live with the couple and traded enough costumes to buy them a modern flat, as well as a taxi for her son-in-law. Customers are now taken by taxi to the flat, where they can browse in comfort rather than bargaining on a street corner. The woman is now saving to send her granddaughter to a private school in Guiyang. Change is not only inevitable but is encouraged by the new entrepreneurial socialism fostered by Chinese government policies. Instead of focusing on their own identity, the Miao are now adapting in order to exploit economic opportunities. The pressures of modernization in Guizhou will continue to have a major impact on the traditional textile cultures of the province.

CHINA

SICHUAN

Chang Jiang (Yangtze)

SICHUAN

ZUNYI

Fanjing
2493 m ▲

Tongren •

TONGREN

BIJIE

• Zunyi

Bijie •

HUNAN

GUIZHOU

Shidong •

Huangping •

Jiuchaiping
2900 m ▲

Weining •

Taijiang •

Jianhe •

Zhijin •

Kaili •

♦ Guiyang

Liupanshui •

• Nankai

Leigong
2178 m ▲

Leishan •

• Shuicheng

Huaxi •

Anshun •

Duyun •

QIANDONGNAN

Liuzhi •

Huishui •

Danzhai •

YUNNAN

ANSHUN

• Sandu

• Rongjiang

Panxian •

QIANNAN

Xingren •

Luodian •

XINGYI

Xingyi •

GUANGXI

Longlin •

♦ province capital
• town
▲ mountain peak

FEMALE FESTIVE COSTUME
Short collared jacket with wide sleeves and attached cape,
dating from the 1920s.

The jacket is made of two narrow widths of hemp cloth, seamed at
the back and sides. Two decorative woven rectangles joined at the centre
back form the cape. The sleeves are simple woven rectangles attached to
the underlayer. The supplementary wool patterning is woven on a
hemp ground and further decorated with applied cloth.
55 × 175 cm (21¾ × 69 in)

THE JACKET BACK HAS A STRONG GEOMETRIC DESIGN PICKED OUT IN WHITE CLOTH EDGED WITH RED. ON THE SHOULDERS IS A ZIGZAG

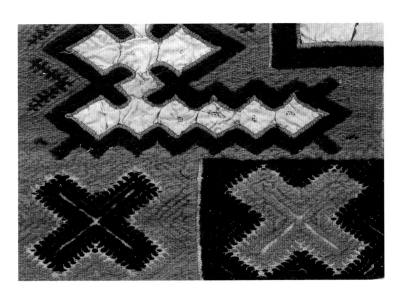

DESIGN IN RED AND BLACK. THE SLEEVE ECHOES THE PATTERNING, BUT ALSO EMPLOYS ASYMMETRY TO CREATE ADDED INTEREST.

FEMALE EVERYDAY/FESTIVE JACKET
Sleeveless cape with collar, tacked to a
collarless underlayer of hemp or ramie.

The decoration is made up of strips of
yellow, red, black, white and blue appliquéd
cotton strips, which surround rectangles and
squares embroidered in white, red and
green cross-stitch motifs.
66 × 73 cm (26 × 28¾ in)

THE DECEPTIVELY COMPLICATED DESIGN
EMPLOYS EMBROIDERED PANELS, FRAMED
WITHIN STRIPED BORDERS. IT IS UNIFIED
BY THE REPETITION OF THE SAME RED AND
GREEN IN BOTH ELEMENTS.

FEMALE FESTIVE JACKET

Long-sleeved jacket in which the front extends to the right side and ties under
the arm. The sides are open and there are five added triangles at each side.

There is an inner lining of chemically dyed blue manufactured cotton.
The back and front yoke is shiny green damask-type weave. The sleeve is
decorated in applied bands of embroidery and cloth. The lower back and front
have applied embroidered pieces worked in satin stitch, edged round the yoke
with bought ribbon. The collar and facing strip is embroidered
with silk in satin stitch over paper.
45 × 115 cm (17¾ × 45¼ in)

THE STRENGTH OF THIS DESIGN LIES IN ITS DIVISION OF SEPARATE AREAS OF
PATTERN. THE DRAMATIC GREEN CENTRE PANEL IS SLASHED BY THE COLLAR AND A
FACING STRIP. BELOW: THE LOWER FRONT PANEL IS RICHLY DECORATED.

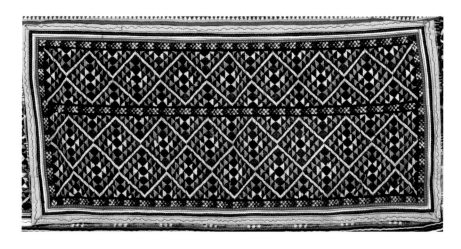

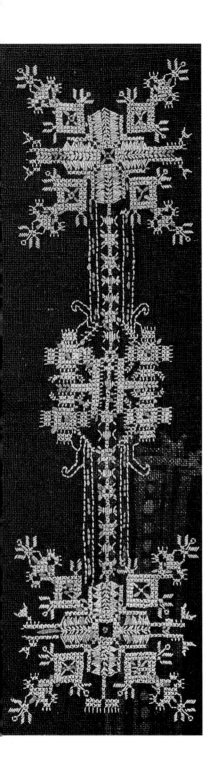

FEMALE FESTIVE JACKET
Back view of a sleeveless jacket, which
has detachable sleeves (not shown).
Rectangular collar, open at one side.
No front opening.

Hand-woven indigo-dyed cotton.
There are shadowy underdesigns of
wax resist on the back, echoing the main
embroidered decoration, which is worked
in silk in cross and associated stitches.
The lower back is framed on three
sides with a border pattern.
82 × 71 cm (32¼ × 28 in)

A CLASSIC GEOMETRIC PATTERN,
BASED ON CRUCIFORMS, CREATES
A SNOWFLAKE-LIKE IMPRESSION
IN IVORY, SOFT PINK AND YELLOW.

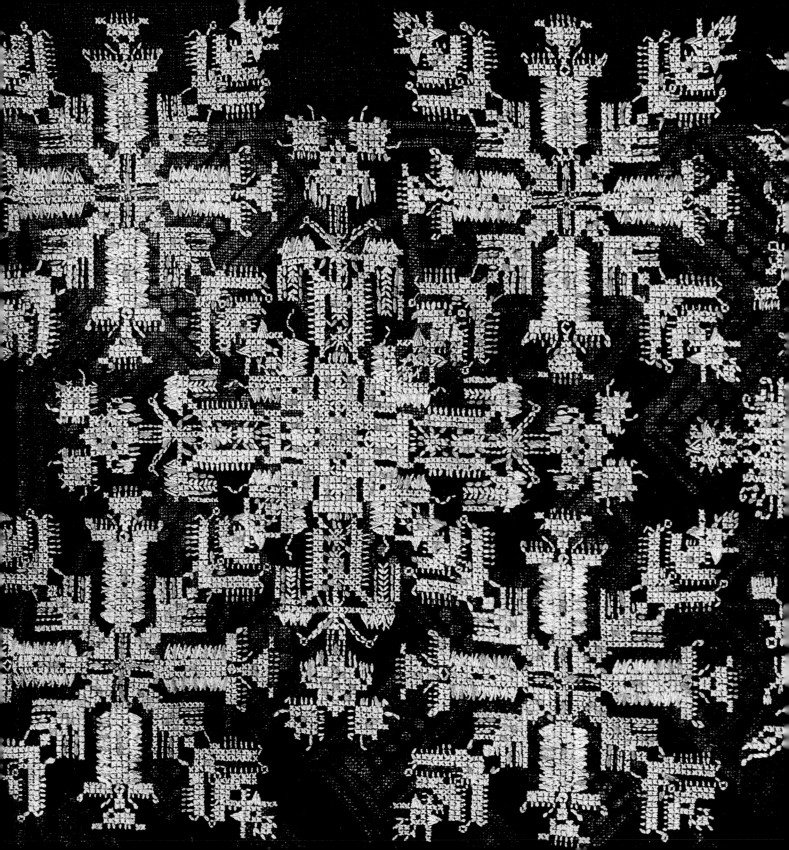

FEMALE FESTIVE JACKET
Short, wide, long-sleeved collared jacket
with centre front opening.

It is decorated with applied rectangles of red
manufactured cotton embroidered with spiral
designs and circles, mainly in yellow
satin stitch and cross stitch.
60 × 172 cm (23¾ × 67¾ in)

THIS DESIGN, WITH PANELS EMBROIDERED IN PIERCINGLY BRIGHT COLOURS, IS
CONTERBALANCED BY AREAS OF PLAIN FABRIC IN MATCHING COLOURS.

THIS DESIGN INTEGRATES TWO TOTALLY DIFFERENT CONTRASTING ELEMENTS. THE LARGE SEMICIRCULAR BACK PANEL AND SLEEVE DETAIL FEATURES A RHYTHM OF CIRCLES AND SPIRALS, IN STARK CONTRAST TO THE BRIGHTLY COLOURED EMBROIDERED BIRDS AND FLOWER DECORATIONS THAT PUNCTUATE THE GARMENT.

FEMALE FESTIVE JACKET
Collared long-sleeved jacket, curved at the bottom edge
and fastened on the right side with a side opening.

The base cloth is hand-woven diamond twill, dyed indigo
with a good sheen on the outside. The upper sleeves and upper back
panels are wax resist. The silk satin epaulets, neck and front facings are
embroidered in satin stitch and outlined with a bound core thread,
couched on. Two small red wool panels in the
lower back are similarly embroidered.
75 × 134 cm (29½ × 52¾ in)

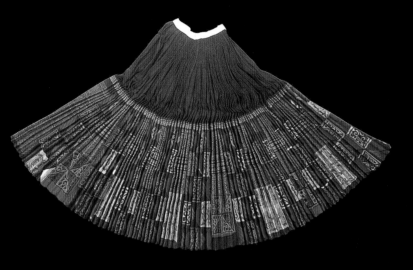

FEMALE SKIRT
Pleated skirt with 45 cm (17¾ in) deep
patchwork band.

The cloth of the lower section is hand-
woven cotton, dyed with indigo. It is stiffened and
forms the base of the patchwork. The upper part is
manufactured cotton dyed black, with an undyed
waistband. All the complete squares are embroidered,
some directly on silk while others have cutaway cloth
designs outlined with couching threads.
79 × 80 cm (31 × 31 ½ in) at waist

THE IMPACT OF THIS DESIGN IS ACHIEVED BY
EMPLOYING A SIMPLE PACHWORK IN WHICH
LARGER PANELS WORK AGAINST THE SMALLER
PATCHES TO CREATE A VIBRANT PATTERN. THE
FLASHES OF RED THROUHOUT SET UP THE EFFECT
OF SYNCOPATED RHYTHM.

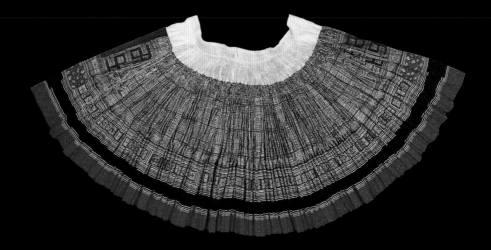

FEMALE FESTIVE SKIRT
A very full gathered skirt.

The top base cloth is hand-woven undyed ramie.
The middle section is manufactured cotton cloth decorated with wax
resist and red and yellow cotton appliqué, and the bottom is a finer indigo-
dyed ramie with multicoloured appliqué, including tiny 'silk felt' pieces.
The bottom of the skirt is red manufactured cotton cloth.
80 × 81 cm (31½ × 32 in) at waist

THE SUCCESS OF THIS DESIGN LIES IN ITS USE OF SMALL INDIVIDUAL PATTERNS
BUILT INTO HORIZONTAL BANDS.

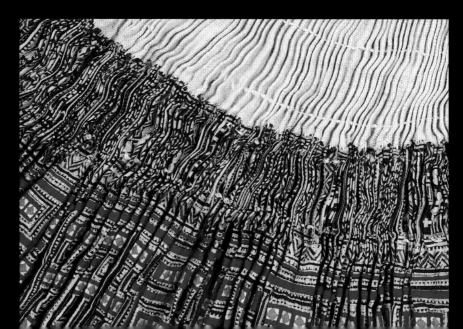

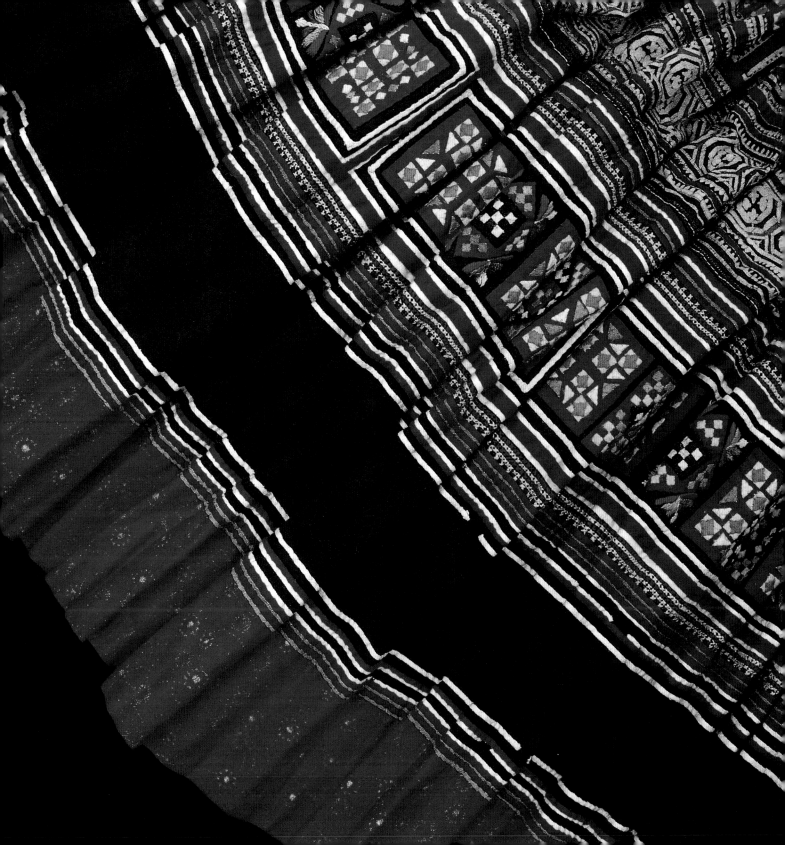

FEMALE FESTIVE JACKET

Short collared jacket, slightly flared at the bottom, with wide
sleeves and front opening. A rare style, probably not worn today, which
according to Chinese sources dates to the late nineteenth century.

The base lining is hand-woven unbleached cotton, the top
layer a patchwork of many different cloths. Both back and front have
horizontal bands of decoration, which include embroidery and
appliqué. The sleeves are banded with appliqué, wax resist,
shiny black cotton and pattern darning.
48.5 × 143.5 cm (19 × 56½ in)

THIS JACKET IS DECORATED
WITH A COMBINATION OF
BOLD GEOMETRIC PANELS
CONTRASTING WITH AREAS
OF INTRICATE WORK.

THE SLEEVE PANEL (LEFT),
WORKED IN WAX RESIST,
FEATURES EIGHT RADIATING
SPIRALS ARRANGED IN A
CIRCLE WITHIN A SQUARE.

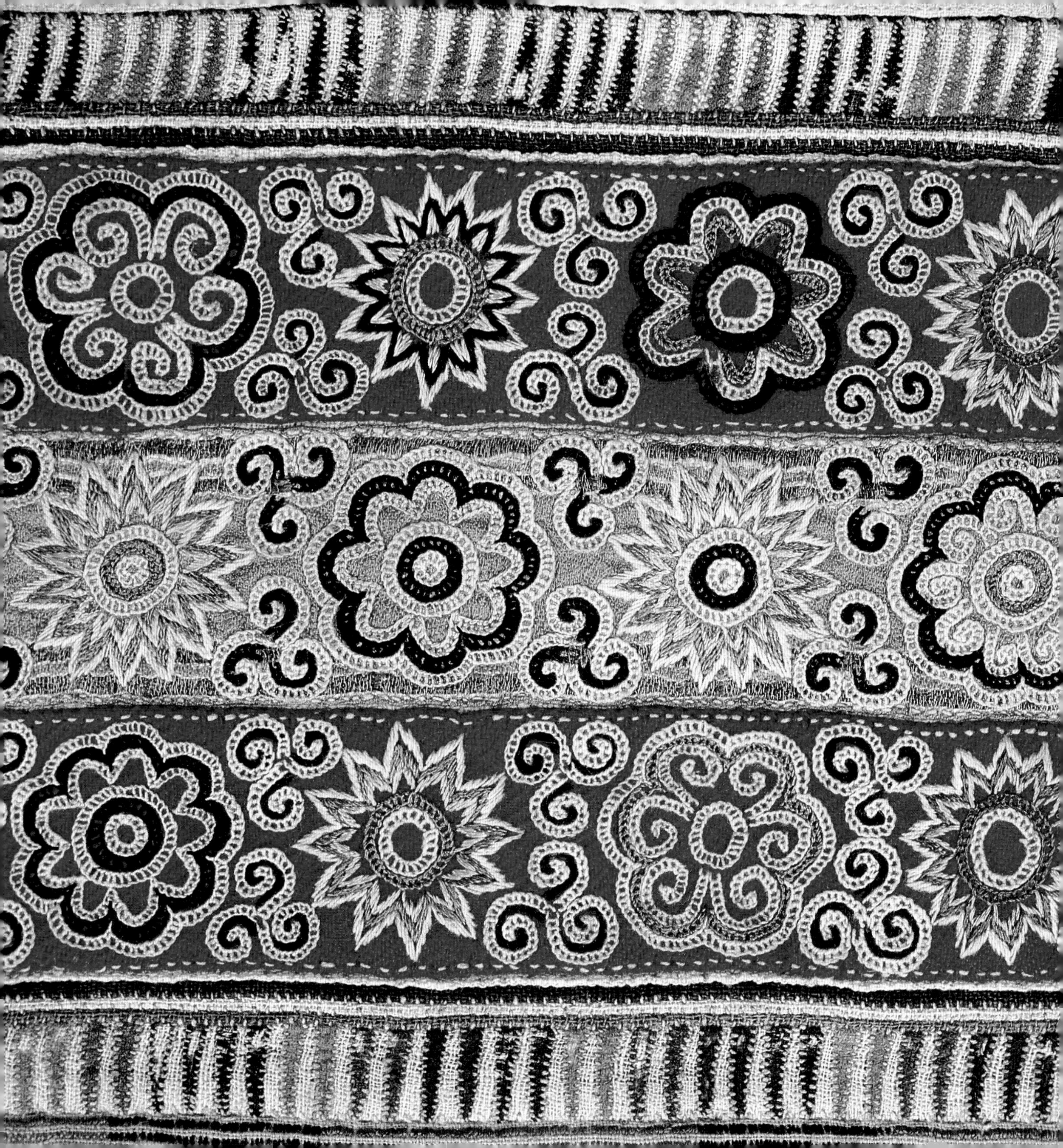

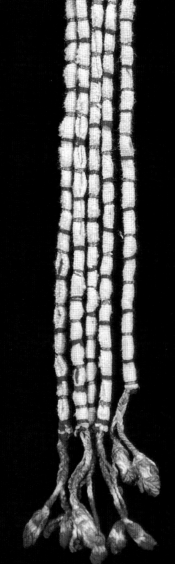

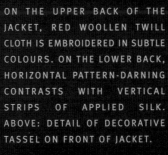

ON THE UPPER BACK OF THE JACKET, RED WOOLLEN TWILL CLOTH IS EMBROIDERED IN SUBTLE COLOURS. ON THE LOWER BACK, HORIZONTAL PATTERN-DARNING CONTRASTS WITH VERTICAL STRIPS OF APPLIED SILK. ABOVE: DETAIL OF DECORATIVE TASSEL ON FRONT OF JACKET.

TYPICAL FEATURES OF THE 'HUNDRED-BIRD COAT' ARE BOLD BIRD MOTIFS WITHIN GEOMETRIC SHAPES. THE 'SKIRT' PANELS ARE EDGED WITH NARROW APPLIED STRIPS OF SHINY DARK INDIGO CLOTH WITH A CUT-

'HUNDRED-BIRD COAT'

Collarless jacket with open sides and sleeves and an attached 'skirt' of thirteen free-hanging panels. Worn at the Guzang festival held by the Miao at irregular intervals to renew and reinforce spiritual links with their ancestors. Probably worn by both men and women over their normal full costume.

The base cloth is undyed hand-woven cotton. It is decorated with applied green sateen and embroidered with floss silk in satin stitch over papercuts in strong colours.
100 × 145 cm (39½ × 57 in)

OUT DIAMOND PATTERN. ON THE ENDS OF THEM ARE SHORT STRINGS OF 'JOB'S TEARS' SEEDS AND CHICKEN FEATHERS. BELOW: THE DESIGN DETAIL ON THE UNDERARM IS A SWASTIKA-TYPE MOTIF ON A PATTERNED WEAVE.

FESTIVAL JACKET
Collarless sleeved jacket with attached
'skirt' of twelve hanging panels, worn over a
complete costume at festivals, probably
by men and women alike.

The base cloth is undyed hand-woven cotton in
diamond twill weave. On the decorated areas are
thin sheets of applied light green 'silk felt'
embroidered with satin-stitch motifs.
135 × 160 cm (53 × 63 in)

OPPOSITE: THE BACK PANEL FEATURES ROWS OF
PAIRED STYLIZED BIRDS SET IN A DIAMOND,
SURROUNDED BY LARGER, MORE ELABORATE BIRD
MOTIFS. THE MUTED COLOURS HARMONIZE THE
VARIOUS ELEMENTS OF THE DESIGN.

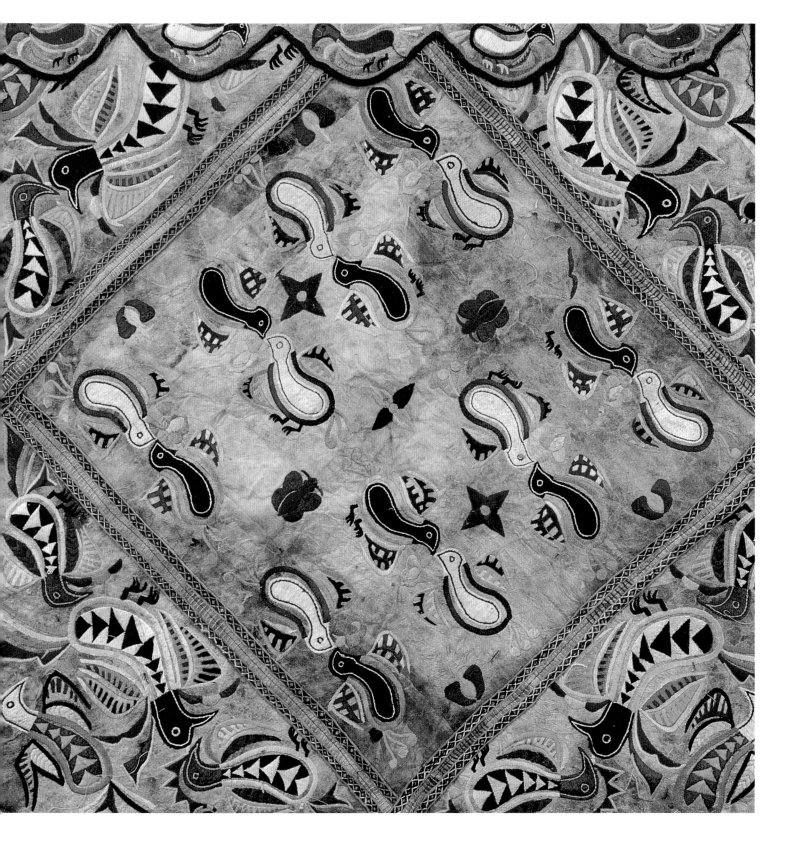

MAN'S FESTIVE JACKET

Collarless short-sleeved and short-waisted
jacket, open at the front, with cuffs, front lapel and
lower back panel embroidered and woven.

The cloth is hand-woven cotton, indigo-dyed to almost
black, with a sheen. The decorated areas are patchwork blocks of
applied decorated material of different types. Various techniques and
motifs are used, including supplementary weft patterned weave,
floral motifs in satin stitch outlined with metal thread,
geometric motifs in satin or cross stitch, and narrow
pieces of applied cloth and 'silk felt'.
43 × 63 cm (17 × 24¾ in)

LIMITED AREAS OF DECOR-
ATION GIVE THIS JACKET
DRAMATIC IMPACT. INTRICATE
AND JEWEL–LIKE SQUARE
BLOCKS OF COLOUR ARE
SUBDIVIDED INTO TRIANGLES

AND SMALLER SQUARES, OR
DECORATED WITH ORGANIC
SCROLL DESIGNS, TO FORM
A HARMONIOUS WHOLE.
THE CUFFS ARE FURTHER
ENHANCED BY SEQUINS.

FEMALE FESTIVE JACKET
Collared jacket with central front opening.
The neck and front facing is continuous, widening
towards the bottom on the left side.

The jacket has an inner and an outer layer. The inner layer
is hand-woven cotton dyed dark indigo, and the outer one
is a figured satin in an aubergine colour. The decorative
areas consist of starched silk rectangles, folded into
triangles and stitched through the points.
93 × 109 cm (36½ × 43 in)

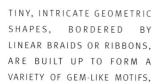

TINY, INTRICATE GEOMETRIC SHAPES, BORDERED BY LINEAR BRAIDS OR RIBBONS, ARE BUILT UP TO FORM A VARIETY OF GEM-LIKE MOTIFS,

NO TWO OF WHICH ARE THE SAME. THE COLOUR IS PRE-DOMINANTLY AZURE BLUE WITH FLASHES OF WHITE, PURPLE AND ORANGE.

WOMAN'S FESTIVE JACKET
Collared jacket with a central front opening, with decoration
on the sleeves, shoulders, neck and front facings.

The base cloth is hand-woven cotton, indigo-dyed to a
dark blue. There is no inner lining. The finely drawn and
detailed decorative panels are embroidered in floss
silk in satin stitch over papercuts.
81 × 130 cm (32 × 51 ¼ in)

THE ZOOMORPHIC MOTIFS, WITH STRONG ANTHROPOMORPHIC OVERTONES, ARE WORKED IN SILVERY SOFT PURPLE AND WATERY PALE BLUE SILKS. THE PLEASING SUBTLETY OF THE COLOURS MAY, HOWEVER, HAVE BEEN ENHANCED AS THE RESULT OF FADING OVER TIME.

THIS VIBRANT DESIGN EMPLOYS RICH REDS AND BLUES IN COMPLEX GEO-METRIC PATTERNS, USING EMBROIDERED STRIPS INTERSPERSED WITH PLAIN, SHINY GREEN SATIN. THE HAND-WOVEN TIES HAVE A WARP-FACED GEOMETRIC PATTERN IN VIVID COLOURS.

FEMALE FESTIVE JACKET

Collared jacket with central front opening, of which the front is longer than the back. The neck and front facing is continuous, widening towards the bottom at the left front.

The inner layer is cotton, dyed locally, and the outer layer is bought figured damask, originally dyed green but now acquiring a metallic bronze hue. The decoration is made up of narrow applied strips of embroidery as well as woven pieces, with weft-faced patterned pieces joined at the selvedges.

83 × 119 cm (32¼ × 46¾in)

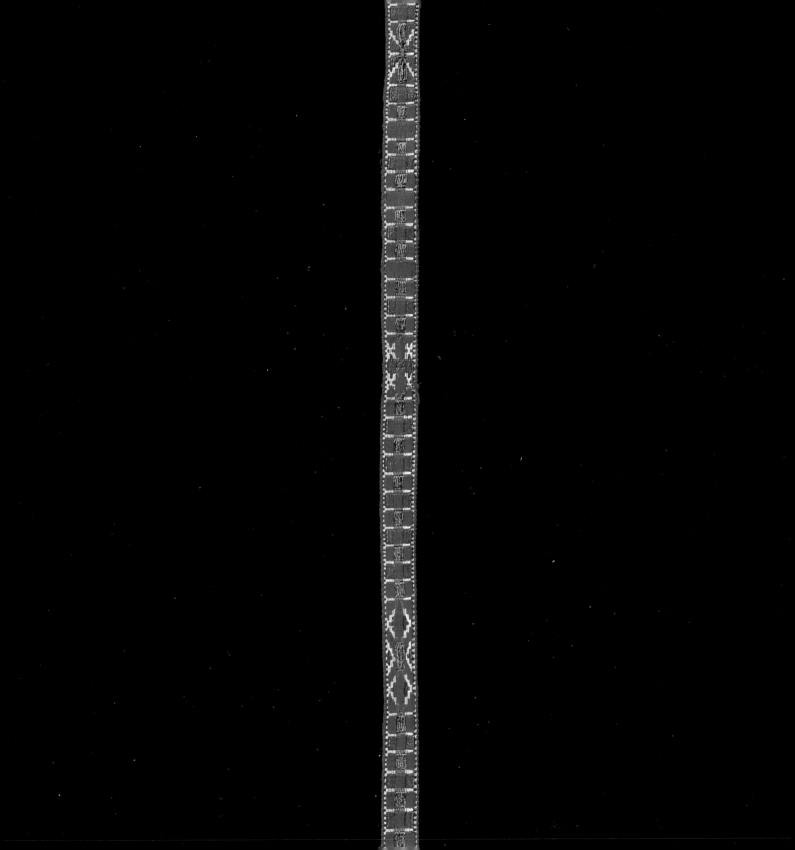

THIS SLEEVE DETAIL REVEALS THE INTRICACY OF THE STITCHWORK. THE BACK OF THE JACKET (OPPOSITE) HAS THE GREATER AREA OF EMBROIDERY AND RELIES ON A LIMITED RANGE OF STRONG COLOURS TO CREATE A HARMONIOUS EFFECT.

FESTIVE APRON
Rectangular front apron with top ties
set in from the side.

The base cloth is hand-woven cotton
dyed dark indigo, on to which a rectangular block of
decoration has been sewn. This consists of numerous
strips of different-coloured satins. Various coloured
geometric motifs have been stitched on to each
strip with dark thread. Some strips are edged
with a folded, wafer-thin, malleable 'metal'
strip, also attached by stitching.
44 × 47 cm (17¼ × 18½ in)

THE OVERALL DESIGN IS BUILT UP FROM REPEATING STRIPS OF HIGHLY COLOURED MATERIAL, SUBTLY DECORATED. THIS INTRICACY CONTRASTS STRONGLY WITH THE BOLD, ALMOST CRUDE, COLOURED 'SILK FELT' FRINGING AT THE BOTTOM OF THE APRON. TWO SINGLE ROWS OF METALLIC STRIPS BIND THE WARP THREADS.

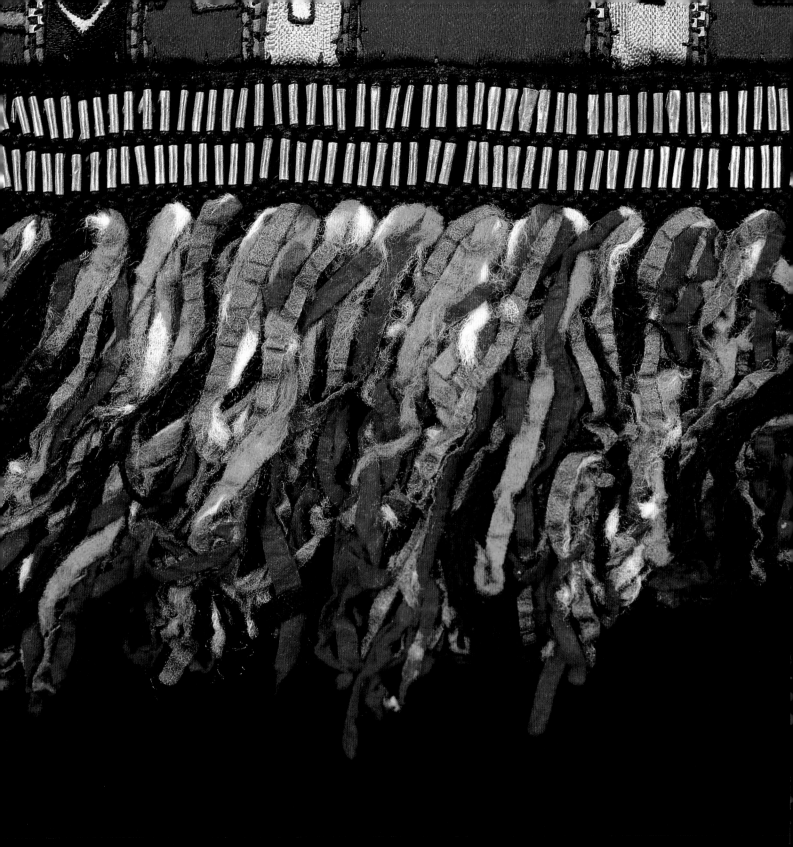

T-SHAPED BABY-CARRIER
The top of the T is extended on either side
by bands that tie around the child's bottom
and are secured at the woman's waist.

The base cloth is a hand-woven
indigo-dyed cotton cloth, which shows no
sign of use. The main decorated panel is
embroidered in counted work and has
probably been remounted.
74 × 98 cm (29¼ × 38½ in)

A CLASSIC STEP-AND-REPEAT DESIGN
FEATURING PAIRS OF STYLIZED BIRDS
INTERSPERSED WITH BUTTERFLY MOTIFS
SET IN HORIZONTAL LINES. THE BIRDS
APPEAR UPSIDE DOWN.

FESTIVE JACKET
Copious jacket with central front opening.
This is not a contemporary garment,
and its provenance is unknown.

The base cloth is coarse hand-woven cotton
and the decoration consists of applied pieces of
silk-like cloth, which are sewn with satin-stitch
motifs in floss silk over papercuts.
60 × 138 cm (23¾ × 54¼ in)

THIS JACKET COMBINES
FREE-FLOWING FORMS
WITHIN A GEOMETRIC
STRUCTURE. THE FRONT
EDGE ONLY HAS A SIMPLE

BORDER (LEFT). THIS HIGHLY
INTRICATE DESIGN WORKS
BY LIMITING THE COLOUR
TO LITTLE MORE THAN
REDS AND PINKS.

FEMALE FESTIVE JACKET
Short-sleeved collared jacket
with front opening.

This may be a modern interpretation of a
traditional style. The decoration is far more elaborate
and colourful than that of the traditional jacket, which has
only a discrete embroidered front and collar strip, and on the
back a single small 'tin'-decorated rectangle, with tassels. The
base cloth is indigo-dyed cotton with a purple sheen. The tiny
tin strips have presumably been stitched on to the base cloth,
and between the tin patterns is coloured embroidery.
Locally these techniques are considered secret,
therefore they cannot be verified.
93 × 101 cm (36¾ × 39¾ in)

THE EFFECT ACHIEVED IS BASED ON THE AMOUNT OF LIGHT
REFLECTED BY THE 'TIN' DECORATION. THE ALMOST BLACK
GROUND FABRIC, TOGETHER WITH THE LIGHT AREAS
COVERED BY THE TIN, CONTRASTS WITH THE COLOURED
EMBROIDERY PANELS. THE THREE ELEMENTS COMBINE TO
PRODUCE A STARTLING DOUBLE-PATTERN EFFECT. THE
LONG FRINGE IS OF TWISTED WARP THREADS AROUND
WHICH ARE WRAPPED TIN STRIPS (SEE RIGHT-HAND PAGE
OVERLEAF).

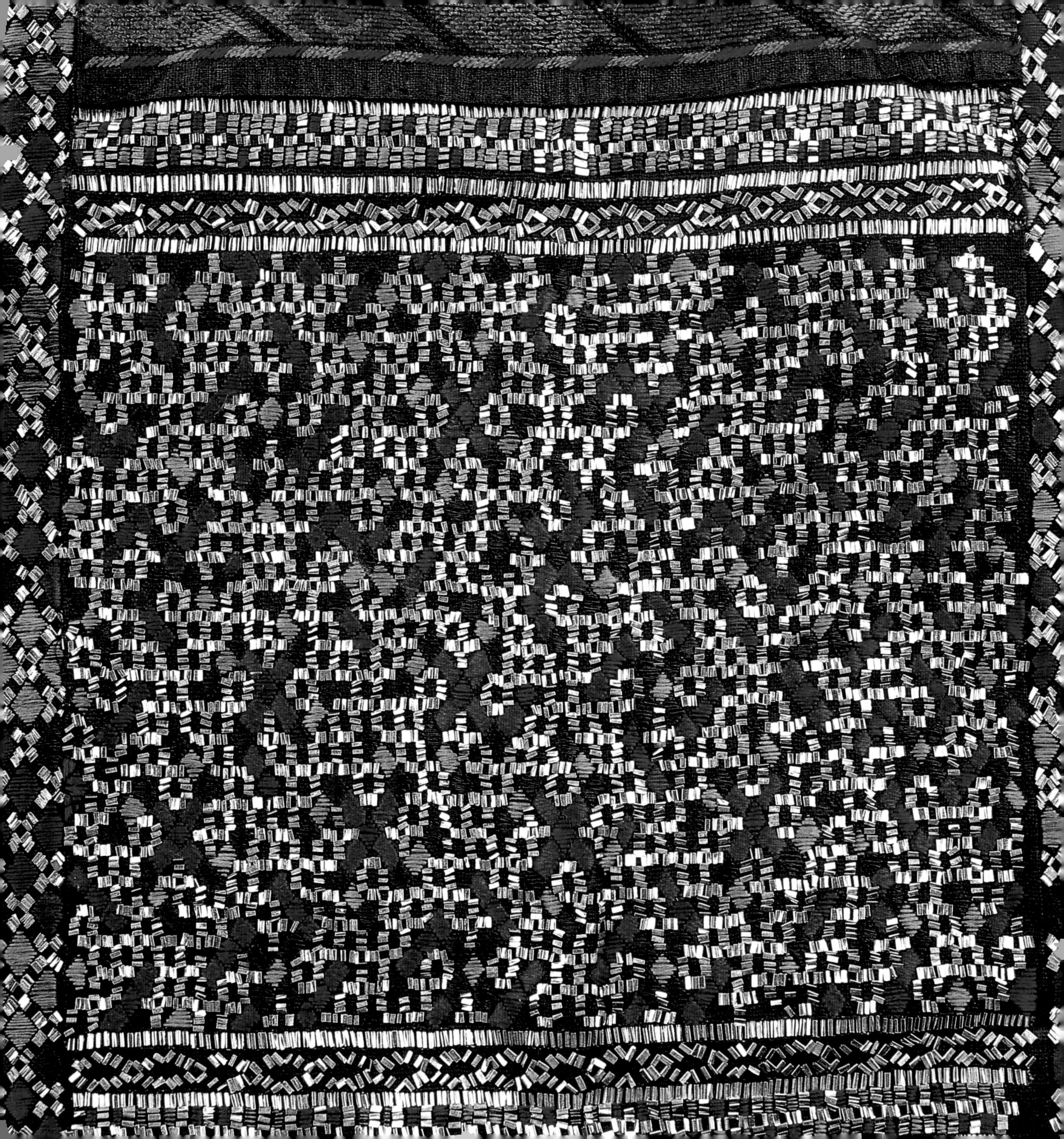

FEMALE FESTIVE JACKET
Sleeved collared jacket with front opening and side slits.
Probably worn by an older woman.

A hand-woven indigo-dyed cotton jacket. The decoration is
applied to the sleeves, shoulders, collar and front facings. The dominant
embroidery is applied braid, which is handmade. Flat braid is used on the
fronts and collar, and pleated braid is applied on the shoulders and
sleeves. Rows of folded silk and gold paper decorate the
collar and edge the braided designs.
96 × 128 cm (37¾ × 50½ in)

THIS STRONG BUT SIMPLE DESIGN USES PANELS OF FLORAL MOTIFS
FRAMED BY INTRICATELY FOLDED SILK EMBROIDERY. SEQUINS HAVE
BEEN ADDED TO OFFSET THE BRAIDING.

FEMALE APRON (GEJIA GROUP)
Squarish apron with hand-woven ties.
Two smaller wax-resist aprons are
usually worn over the top.

The base material is blue
cotton, indigo dyed. It is embroidered
in cross and associated stitches.
42 × 39 cm (16½ × 15¼ in)

THIS SIMPLE, IF INTRICATE, DESIGN REVOLVES AROUND FOUR CRUCIFORM SHAPES SET ON A GEOMETRICALLY PATTERNED BACKGROUND. ADDITIONAL IMPACT IS

ACHIEVED BY ALLOWING THE DARK BLUE GROUND (WHICH IN PLACES IS ALSO EMBROIDERED IN DARK BLUE) TO PICK OUT IMPORTANT ELEMENTS.

FEMALE FESTIVE JACKET (GEJIA GROUP)
Slim-fitting long-sleeved jacket
with stand-up collar and front opening.

The jacket is made of cotton, decorated using the
wax-resist technique, and dyed in indigo.
81 × 136 cm (32 × 53½ in)

AN ELEGANT GARMENT
INCORPORATING TWO
CONTRASTING DESIGN
ELEMENTS: VERY BOLD
FOLIATE-PATTERNED
FRONT PANELS AND
SUBTLER GEOMETRICALLY
PATTERNED SLEEVE PANELS,
CLEVERLY INTEGRATED
BY THE SIMPLEST USE
OF WHITE ON INDIGO.

BABY-CARRIER (GEJIA GROUP)
T-shape baby-carrier with attached bands
that pass across the chest, round the waist and
under the child's bottom and are tied at the front.

Indigo-dyed cotton, predominantly embroidered in a chain
stitch filled with satin stitch, worked with a twisted
thread. The tying bands are decorated with what may
be a paste-resist design, of birds and flowers.
67 × 64 cm (26½ × 25¼ in)

THIS DENSELY PATTERNED DESIGN UTILIZES A SEEMINGLY ENDLESS REPETITION OF
THE SAME BASIC MOTIFS, WITH TINY MODIFICATIONS. IT SUCCEEDS BY EMPLOYING
JUST THREE CLOSELY RELATED COLOURS AGAINST A DARK GROUND.

WOMAN'S HAT (GEJIA GROUP)
This style of hat is worn on market days and at festivals.

A flat-topped headpiece with an outer row of
shiny beads and a distinctive bright red fringe. It
rests on an undercap of cotton, decorated in wax resist,
which covers the ears and the back of the head
and is held in place by a long silver hatpin.
height 25 cm, diameter 14.5 cm (9¾ × 5¾ in)

ON THIS HAT A DRAMATICALLY BEADED DISC AND FLAMBOYANT
FRINGE CONTRAST WITH THE SIMPLICITY OF THE BLUE AND
WHITE UNDERCAP.

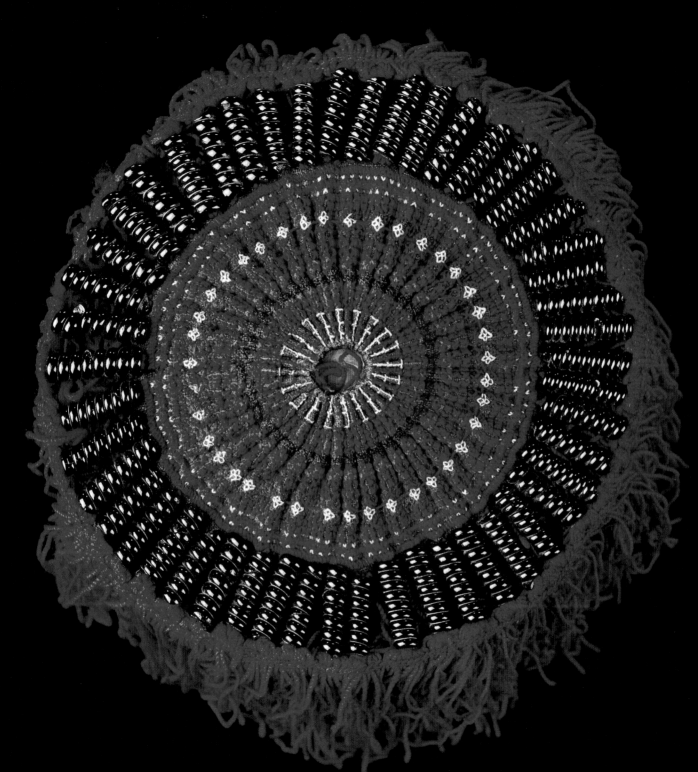

FEMALE FESTIVE JACKET
Sleeved, collared jacket with front opening
and side slits.

The outer cloth is hand-woven indigo-
dyed cotton with an alternating float weave to
give a spiralling four-key design. The decoration,
worked in satin stitch, is applied to the sleeves,
shoulders, collar and front facings.
94 × 124 cm (37 × 48¾ in)

A PERFECT EXAMPLE OF
FLAMBOYANT JACKET
DESIGN. THE CONCISE
TRADITIONAL COLLAR
DECORATION, CONSIST-
ING OF MANY LINES OF
FOLDED SILK TRIANGLES,
CONTRASTS WITH THE

EXUBERANT DESIGN ON
THE SLEEVES, DOMINATED
BY A BRIGHTLY COLOURED
DRAGON, WATER BUFFALO
AND BUTTERFLY INTER-
WOVEN WITH FLORAL
MOTIFS, ON A DEEP
BLUE GROUND.

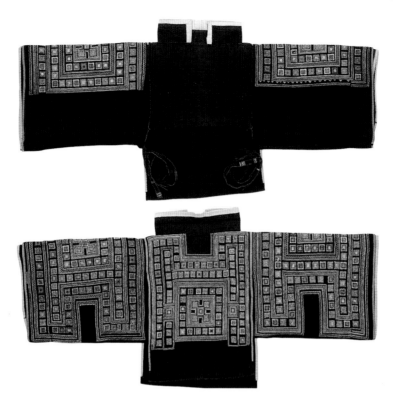

FEMALE FESTIVE JACKET
Collared outer jacket with a highly decorative
embroidered back and very deep sleeves.

The base cloth is hand-woven cotton,
indigo-dyed to dark blue. The back and sleeves are embroidered
with cross and associated stitches in silk.
61 × 126 cm (24 × 49½ in)

THE VISUAL COHESION
OF THE OVERALL DESIGN
IS PROVIDED BY SUBTLY
VARYING SQUARES, EACH
OF WHICH IS INTRICATELY

WORKED. THE CENTRAL
BACK PANEL (OPPOSITE)
FEATURES A SIMPLE CRUCI-
FORM SHAPE ENCLOSED
BY THREE BORDERS.

glossary

aniline dye synthetic dye made from coal tar

anthropomorphic in a shape or form that represents people or human features

appliqué decorative technique of attaching pieces of contrasting material to a fabric, usually by stitching

body-tensioned loom simple portable loom, traditionally used by women in various parts of the world since earliest times. The WARP is spread out on two rods and tensioned between the weight of the woman's body at one end and a fixed point (on a post or tree) at the other. Also known as a back-strap loom.

braiding technique of making decorative braid in the form of a narrow cord, by interweaving or plaiting threads; also the braid itself, used to trim garments and textiles

calender to beat cloth in order to give it a smooth or glazed surface finish

chain stitch rings of thread linked together in a chain

couching fixing a thread (or cord) to a fabric by stitching it down flat with another, usually finer, thread

damask figured woven fabric with a pattern visible on both sides

figured patterned or decorated with a design

float weave weave in which the WEFT passes over a number of warps to form a pattern

floss silk loosely plied silk thread used for embroidery

gaiter a single piece of seamed cloth worn as a covering for the leg, from knee to ankle

ginning removing the seeds from raw cotton with a machine called a gin

heddles loops or rigid structures on a loom through which the warp threads are passed to form the SHED; each warp is threaded through the eye of a heddle

hemp tough-fibred Asian plant (*Cannabis sativa*) used to make yarn that is woven into cloth

Job's tears tropical grass (*Coix lacryma-jobi*) from Southeast Asia, which bears hard, shiny seed-holding structures that are used as decorative beads

lusheng pipes traditional bamboo reed pipes played by the Miao

Mao suit style of jacket and trousers associated with revolutionary China, taking its name from Chairman Mao

papercuts pieces of paper with patterns drawn on them (often stitched through to create the design and left on the finished garment)

pattern darning counted-thread technique worked in a running stitch, used for geometric designs

phyllomorphic in a shape or form that represents plants

pick a single throw of the weft from one selvedge to the other

plain weave balanced weave in which the weft alternates over and under the warp; also called tabby weave

puttee A long cloth strip wound round the leg from ankle to knee

ramie woody Asian plant (*Boehmeria nivea*) of the nettle family, from which yarn is made for weaving into cloth, cord, etc; the word is also used to mean the cloth itself

resist see WAX RESIST, ETC

reverse appliqué variation of APPLIQUÉ, where the decorative addition consists of two pieces of fabric. One is first tacked on top of the other, a design is cut out of the top piece only, and the cut edges are then turned under and hemmed to expose the bottom layer.

running stitch stitch that involves taking the needle and thread through the cloth at regularly spaced intervals, so that it appears the same on both sides

sateen woven fabric with a glossy, satin-like finish

satin stitch long, straight embroidery stitch where each stitch is worked parallel to and touching the next, usually across the shape of a particular design motif

selvedge (or selvage) the non-fraying edge of a piece of cloth

shafts the slats of wood on a treadle loom that support the HEDDLES

shed the gap between the WARP threads on a loom through which the WEFT is passed during weaving

smocking gathering material into tight pleats, which are then stitched together

splicing joining technique whereby two lengths of plant fibre (for example) are laid end to end and the strands splayed out and then twisted together, or interwoven, to form a strong joint

supplementary weft a contrasting (and sometimes thicker) ornamental thread added to the ground yarn to form a woven design

swastika equal-armed cross with the ends of each arm extended at opposite right angles

swidden land cleared for cultivation by slashing and burning the existing vegetation

treadle loom sturdy floor loom on which threads are raised and lowered by means of shafts attached to treadles, which increases the speed of weaving in comparison to the BODY-TENSIONED LOOM

twill weave woven fabric with a surface of parallel ridges, achieved by passing each WEFT thread over two and under one, moving to right or left on each successive pick. A diagonal, chevron or diamond pattern can be produced by adjusting the sequencing.

warp the longitudinal threads in a woven structure

warp beam beam on which the warp is wound, located at the back of a treadle loom

warp-faced with the warp threads predominating over the weft (which is almost obscured)

wax resist, stitch resist, paste resist design techniques that involve preventing certain areas of a fabric from accepting the dye. The design is drawn in a dye-resistant substance known as a resist (such as wax or paste), or worked in stitches, so that after the dyeing it is still the same colour and stands out against the dyed areas.

weft the thread that is passed from SELVEDGE to selvedge in a woven structure

weft-faced with the weft threads predominating over the warp

whipped sewn or gathered with overcast stitches

zoomorphic in a shape or form that represents animals

selected reading

Baker, M., 'A steep learning curve: Teaching techniques from south-west China,' *The World of Embroidery*, vol. 50, no. 4, July 1999, pp. 232–3.

Balfour-Paul, J., *Indigo*, British Museum Press, 1998.

Boudot, E., 'Minor costumes and textiles of southwestern China,' *Orientations*, vol. 25, no. 2, Feb. 1994, pp. 59–66.

Cheng Weiji (Chief Compiler), *History of Textile Technology of Ancient China*, The Science Press, New York, 1992.

China House Gallery, *Richly Woven Traditions: Costumes of the Miao of Southwest China and Beyond*, The China Institute of America, New York, 1988.

Clarke, S.R., *Among the Tribes of South-West China*, China Inland Mission, Morgan & Scott, London, 1911.

Corrigan, G., 'Geographer turns textile enthusiast in China', *Embroidery*, vol. 45, no. 2, summer 1994, pp. 98–9.

Guizhou: Odyssey Illustrated Guide, The Guidebook Company, Hong Kong, 1995.

'Guizhou province, south-west China: Bast fibres used by the Miao and the processes involved', *Newsletter of the Textile Society of Hong Kong*, vol. 4, no. 3, May 1996, pp. 3–5.

'Search and research: The pleated skirts of the Miao', *The World of Embroidery*, vol. 49, no. 1, Jan. 1998, pp. 10–12.

'Hemp and ramie in southwest China', *Hali*, issue 113, Nov./Dec. 2000.

Cultural Palace of Nationalities, *Clothing and Ornaments of China's Miao People*, Nationality Press, Beijing, 1985.

Garrett, V.M., *Traditional Chinese Clothing in Hong Kong and South China 1840–1980*, Oxford University Press, Hong Kong, 1989.

Chinese Clothing: An Illustrated Guide, Oxford University Press, Hong Kong, 1994.

Gillow, J. and B. Sentance, *World Textiles: A Visual Guide to Traditional Techniques*, Thames & Hudson, London, 1999.

Kuhn, D., *Science and Civilisation in China, 5 IX, Textile Technology: Spinning and Reeling*, Cambridge University Press, Cambridge, 1988.

Laumann, Maryta (ed.), *Miao Textile Design*, Fu Jen Catholic University Press, Taipei, 1993.

O'Connor, D., *Miao Costumes from Guizhou Province*, James Hockey Gallery, West Surrey College of Art & Design, Farnham, 1994.

'Using Hemp in Guizhou Province, south-west China', *Journal for Weavers, Spinners and Dyers*, 170, June 1994, pp. 26–8.

'Best bib and tucker: Embroidery on Miao jackets from Guizhou Province', *Embroidery*, vol. 45, no. 3, autumn 1994, pp. 152–4.

'Textiles of the Miao minority, Guizhou Province, south-west China', *The Textile Society Magazine*, vol. 21, spring/summer 1994, pp. 11–13.

Parsons, K.R., Notes on articles and photographs of the Chinese people of south-west China, British Museum archives (unpublished).

Pollard, S., *The Sam Pollard 'Omnibus': Tight Corners on China — The Story of the Miao in Unknown China*, Woodburn Press, Pennsylvania, 1996.

Rossi, G., 'Traditional cross-stitch among China's remote southwest provinces', *Counted Thread*, June 1986, pp. 3–5.

'A flourishing art — China: Guizhou women continue to embroider their legends', *Threads*, issue 9, Feb./March 1987, pp. 30–32.

'Miao needlework', *Needlework & Thread*, May/June
 1987, pp. 42–4.
'Enduring dress of the Miao: Guizhou Province',
 Ornament, spring 1988, pp. 26–32.

Seiler-Baldinger, A., *Textiles: A Classification of Techniques*,
 Crawford House Press, Bathurst, 1994.
Shanghai Theatrical College (Editorial Committee),
 Ethnic Costumes and Clothing Decorations from China,
Hai Feng Publishing Company Ltd, Sichuan People's
Publishing House, Chengdu, 1986.

Wang, Y., *Chinese Folk Embroidery*, Commercial Press,
 Hong Kong, 1987.

NOTE: *Chinese publications can be obtained by mail
order from Hanshan Tang Books (tel: 020 8788 4464,
fax: 020 8780 1565, email: hst@hanshan.com).*

museum accession numbers

PAGE	ACC. NO.
2	1998 As 1.283
4	1998 As 1.377
7	1998 As 1.388 (top)
7	1998 As 1.340 (left)
7	1998 As 1.291 (right)
7	1998 As 1.334 (below)
23	1977 As 1.20a
24	1998 As 1.242
27	1998 As 1.198
28	1998 As 1.327
31	1998 As 1.322
33	1998 As 1.67
35	1998 As 1.15
36	1998 As 1.35
39	1998 As 1.33
43	1998 As 1.175
46	1998 As 1.182
49	1998 As 1.263
51	1998 As 1.334
53	1998 As 1.357
54	1998 As 1.340
58	1998 As 1.142
61	1998 As 1.338
62	1998 As 1.183
64	1998 As 1.91
69	1998 As 1.376
70	1998 As 1.291
73	1998 As 1.285
74	1998 As 1.294
76	1998 As 1.284
78	1998 As 1.358
81	1998 As 1.138
INSIDE COVER	1998 As 1.377

publisher's acknowledgements

The textiles featured in this book are drawn from the collections of the British Museum's Department of Ethnography and have been selected from the viewpoint of their design and technical merit.

We should like to express our thanks to the many people who have helped us in the production of this book, and in particular from the Museum staff: Helen Wolfe, Imogen Laing and Mike Row. Paul Welti, the art director, must be credited not only for his arresting juxtaposition of illustrations and text, but also for his contribution to the captions analyzing the designs.

author's acknowedgements

I would like to thank Deryn O'Connor and my husband Peter Corrigan for reading the text and offering valuable comments, and Ann Hecht for checking the glossary. I am also most grateful for the assistance provided by my Chinese colleagues and translators, Wang Jun and Lu Chang.

All place names in this book conform to the Pinyin spelling in the *Atlas of the People's Republic of China*, Foreign Language Press, Beijing, 1989.

index